BRUCE & STAN'S™

POCKET GUIDE TO

TALKING WITH GOD

BRUCE BICKEL and STAN JANTZ

HARVEST HOUSE PUBLISHERS
Eugene, Oregon 97402

Cover by Left Coast Design, Portland, Oregon

Cover illustration by Krieg Barrie Illustrations, Hoquiam, Washington

BRUCE & STAN'S POCKET GUIDE TO TALKING WITH GOD
Copyright © 2000 by Bruce Bickel and Stan Jantz
Published by Harvest House Publishers
Eugene, Oregon 97402

Library of Congress Cataloging-in-Publication Data

Bickel, Bruce, 1952-
    [Pocket guide to talking with God]
    Bruce & Stan's pocket guide to talking with God / Bruce Bickel and
    Stan Jantz.
       p. cm.
    ISBN 0-7369-0245-7
    1. Prayer—Christianity. I. Title: Bruce and Stan's pocket guide to
talking with God. II. Jantz, Stan, 1952- III. Title.
BV210.2 .B53 2000
248.3′2—dc21   99-089319

Printed in the United States of America.

00 01 02 03 04 05 06 07 08 09 / BP / 10 9 8 7 6 5 4 3 2 1

Contents

A Note from the Authors

Pick up the phone and call any big company. No longer does some switchboard operator greet you with a friendly voice and connect you with the appropriate department to handle your inquiry. No, that way is too personal (and inefficient). An automated message machine will now answer your call, and you'll eventually abandon all hope of speaking to a human after punching numbers and the "pound key" until your finger is a bloody stub.

If it is that difficult to call your credit-card company about an error on the monthly statement, is it reasonable to think that we can speak directly with God Almighty? Isn't He a little too busy with wars, natural disasters, and the other six billion people on the earth to allow us voice-activated access to Him whenever we want (and without any long-distance collect calling codes to memorize)? In this age of advanced technological telecommunication, it seems unrealistic that we can bypass celestial voice mail and chat personally with the

Creator of the universe, but that's exactly what the Bible says we can do.

The fact that you are reading this introduction tells us that you are interested in talking to God. We will explore with you the process of how prayer works, using the following guidelines:

- **We'll use the Bible for our source of information about prayer.** Oh, sure, we'll include a few pithy quotes and insights from other people and ourselves along the way, but the Bible serves as the foundation for what we discuss. The Bible has centuries of credibility. It is universally recognized as a holy book and contains hundreds of predictions which have come true. It even claims to be the very Word of God:

  > *All Scripture is inspired by God and is useful to teach us what is true* (2 Timothy 3:16).

- **We'll keep it simple and practical.** That's the kind of guys we are—practically simple. We have read a lot of theology books, but most of them don't translate well into everyday living. We'll be discussing the real-life aspects of prayer, whether you are in the boardroom or the bedroom, and whether you are worried about your budget or your bunions.

- **We won't get preachy on you.** Nothing will be crammed down your throat. We aren't trying to decide anything for you. We will give you some things to think about, and you can take it from there.

This Book Is for You If . . .

Prayer is a subject that mystifies everyone. Don't feel embarrassed if you have honest questions about how it works. You aren't alone in your search for meaningful conversation with God. In fact, this book is written with you in mind if . . .

- ✔ You are seeking God, but you haven't connected with Him yet.

- ✔ You want to talk to God, but you aren't sure what to say (or wonder if you have to speak with a Shakespearean accent).

✔ You make the same simple request of God each day, but you still haven't won the lottery.

✔ God didn't seem to pay attention to your desperate prayer during a tragedy in your life, and you haven't bothered talking to him since.

✔ You are a longtime God-follower, but your prayers seem as stale as Aunt Winnie's Christmas fruitcake.

✔ You try to pray each day, but you can't stay mentally focused (because as soon as your eyes are closed, you're thinking about the Seinfeld rerun you watched last night).

How to Use This Book

The obvious approach for using this book requires that you read it. But we'll try to help with certain icons in the margin:

Big Idea—For you readers who skim the text like Stan, this icon alerts you to slow down because an important concept is being discussed. (For you readers who plod along one word at a time like Bruce, you can keep reading at your usual pace.)

Key Verse—We aren't implying that some Bible verses are important and others are not. It's just that some are more famous than others, and we think that the verses marked with this icon will be of particular interest to you.

 Glad You Asked—We think we know what questions you are likely to have because we have asked the same questions ourselves.

 It's a Mystery—We are quick to admit that we don't know everything. When it comes to God, no one does.

 Learn the Lingo—We try to stay away from words we can't spell or pronounce, but if we get too deep into terminology, we make sure we explain it.

 Dig Deeper—At the end of each chapter, we'll give you a list of several books that go into greater detail than what we have discussed.

Beginning at page 107, we have a few "Think About It" questions for each chapter. We intend these to be thought-provoking, chin-scratching, brow-furrowing questions to help you think through what you are learning about prayer. There is no "wrong" answer, and your responses won't be graded, so have fun with the questions. You might even want to discuss these questions with other people in a group (but it will help if you all read the book).

One Final Word Before You Read On

What we say to you won't change your life in any way. However, if you learn about talking to God, and if you start doing it, your entire life can be transformed. But this isn't our guarantee; it is God's promise to you:

> *The earnest prayer of a righteous person has great power and wonderful results* (James 5:16).

We can't do your praying for you; you'll have to do that yourself. But if you are having trouble talking with God, then hopefully we can be of some help to you. Just keep on reading.

Chapter 1

WHY PRAY AT ALL: DOES IT REALLY MAKE A DIFFERENCE?

> *Too many people pray like little boys who knock at doors, then run away.*
>
> —Anonymous

BRUCE & STAN SAY

You make a wish when you blow out the candles on your birthday cake, but you don't really expect your wish will come true. You might have a rabbit's foot on your key chain, but you know it won't bring you good luck. You might even throw a few pennies in the wishing well, but you do it only to get rid of the loose change in your pockets.

Is prayer any different? Do you really expect that something will happen, or is it just a quaint ritual that you do without any expectation of results?

Before we spend any time talking about how to pray or what to pray for, let's discuss whether praying makes any difference at all. If it doesn't really do any good, then let's forget about it. On the other hand, if it can make a difference, then maybe we all have some catching up to do.

Bruce & Stan

Chapter 1

Why Pray at All: Does It Really Make a Difference?

What's Ahead

➤ If God says so, who are you to argue?
➤ Pray for a change
➤ Can you spare the change?
➤ You'll be wasting your breath unless . . .

You probably wanted us to start this book by telling you what to say in your prayers. Well, that won't happen until chapter 3 (sort of), and don't you dare skip ahead. Before you start worrying about *what* to say, you should think about *why* you should even bother with praying. After all, if it doesn't make a difference to anyone, you could ditch the whole concept and save a few moments out of your busy day.

There are lots of *wrong* reasons for praying:

✔ Praying because your saintly great-grandmother used to do it. (She also used to churn butter and darn her own socks. You don't live in a sod house on the prairie just because she did, so don't pray just because she did.)

✔ A psychiatrist costs $175 per hour, but God is free. (God may be interested in hearing about your problems, but not if you only think of Him as cheap therapy.)

✔ You've made a huge mess of your life, and you're yelling at God because you don't want to blame yourself.

✔ You are desperate for money, and you've got no one else to turn to. (Don't expect to get much from God. He saw you rubbing that lamp hoping for a genie before you tried praying.)

✔ Everyone else at church does it (or at least pretends to), and you don't want any of them to think that you are a spiritual sluggard.

> Many people hope that prayer works so they won't have to.

Setting aside the wrong reasons to pray, let's think about the right ones. The most logical reason to pray is that it works—that it makes some kind of difference for you, or other people, or even God. We'll talk about whether prayer makes a difference a little later in this chapter, but let's start off with the single most important reason to pray: God says that we should pray.

If God Says So, Who Are You to Argue?

God doesn't beat around a burning bush when it comes to prayer. He says that we are to do it! Sometimes the Bible is blunt about it, with verses like:

> *Pray at all times* (Ephesians 6:18).

In other verses, the Bible is a little more flowery:

> *Let us come boldly to the throne of our gracious God* (Hebrews 4:16).

Sometimes the Bible verses are instructional:

> *One day Jesus told his disciples a story to illustrate their need for constant prayer and to show them that they must never give up* (Luke 18:1).

Other times, we learn the importance of prayer by the example of others, as when the prophet Samuel said:

> *I will certainly not sin against the L*ORD *by ending my prayers for you* (1 Samuel 12:23).

Often the encouragement to pray is subtly implied by the promised results:

> *The L*ORD *will answer when I call to him* (Psalm 4:3).

But regardless of the style, the instruction is plain and clear:

> *Devote yourselves to prayer* (Colossians 4:2).

> *Always be prayerful* (Romans 12:12).

The emphasis is so great that it is accurate to say that God *commands* us to pray to Him.

You might ask, "Well, why should I do what God says?" We are quick to answer, "Because He is God, and you aren't!" God's nature is perfect, so He couldn't ask us to do anything that would be harmful for us. If He commands us to pray, it must be for our own good. So we should do it because He says to, whether we understand the benefits or not.

God doesn't give us alternative options in this regard. He wants us talking to Him, and He doesn't let us off the hook if we are tired, or if we feel awkward about it, or if we can't think of what to say, or even if things are going fine. All of those factors are irrelevant. He wants us talking to Him.

God doesn't ask us to pray just because He is lonesome. (Don't flatter yourself. He's not lonely, and you are not that great of a conversationalist.) God wants you praying because it is part of the process that He uses to be involved in your life:

✔ God's forgiveness of your sins involves prayer.

✔ Your eternal salvation involves prayer.

✔ You gain spiritual strength through prayer.

✔ You are equipped to resist temptation through prayer.

✔ God may give you wisdom if you pray for it.

✔ Prayer plays a part in physical healing.

Since God created everything, He could have devised any system that He wanted. He chose to use prayer, and we will be missing out on a lot of what He can do for us if we don't get with His program.

Pray for a Change

If God telling you to pray isn't a good enough reason for you (wow, you're tough!), the Bible has another one: Pray because it works. Things can change if you pray.

IT'S NOT ALL ABOUT YOU

In chapter 2, we'll discuss how prayer is simply the conversation you have with God once you have established a personal relationship with Him. Even though prayer can bring changes, God is going to get pretty tired of your prayers if you talk just about what you want Him to change for you: ". . . and please give me more money, and please change my boss's attitude toward me, and please change the weather to give me a nice weekend, and please make me taller." (Okay, so maybe only Bruce makes the last request.)

You wouldn't enjoy a relationship with someone who only liked you for the favors you did for him. God is the same way. He wants your prayers—your conversations with Him— to be primarily about your relationship with each other. Change should be the result of your prayers, not the purpose of your prayers.

Prayer Changes God. There is an interesting story in the Old Testament about King Hezekiah. (If you're looking for a unique name for your baby, you may want to consider this one.) Hezekiah was a good king, but he had a fatal sickness. God's prophet Isaiah came to Hezekiah and said:

> *This is what the LORD says: "Set your affairs in order, for you are going to die. You will not recover from this illness"* (2 Kings 20:1).

(Isaiah could have used a little work on his bedside manner.) King Hezekiah wasn't ready to move from the throne to the tomb, but this was in the days before HMOs, life-support systems, and the Michael Jackson Oxygenation Chamber. So he prayed to God. Back comes Isaiah with a new message from the Lord:

> *The LORD . . . says: "I have heard your prayer. . . . I will heal you. . . . I will add fifteen years to your life"* (2 Kings 20:5-6).

So do you think that prayer can change God's mind? Well, we're sure that Hezekiah thought so because he recovered from his illness and lived for 15 more years. (And while the Bible doesn't record it, we believe he bought a lot of life insurance in the fourteenth year.)

Hezekiah isn't the only example of a situation when God "changed His mind." You can see the same principle in situations such as:

- God was going to obliterate the Israelites for worshiping the golden calf, but Moses prayed for them to be spared and God recanted (Deuteronomy 9:7-19).

- God was going to kill Aaron for leading the Israelites astray, but God spared him as the result of Moses' prayer (Deuteronomy 9:20).

- God sent an angel to destroy Jerusalem and its citizens as punishment for King David's sin. Just in the nick of time, David repented and asked God to spare the people of Jerusalem. God relented in response to David's prayer (1 Chronicles 21:14-28).

 We don't know how this "changing the mind of God" deal works. Nobody does. But this mystery involves the concept of God knowing everything (being "omniscient"). Before the world was created, He knew everything that would happen in our lives. He knows what we will be praying about before we even utter the words. So do our prayers really change what God is going to do if He has known all along that He would be doing what we prayed for? See, we told you it was confusing. But it's a God thing, so don't try to figure it out. You don't have to understand how it works to enjoy the benefits of it (which is the same way we feel about our cars and our computers).

CAN YOU CHANGE THE UNCHANGEABLE?

One of the great personality traits of God is His immutability—He never changes. He remains the same from eternity past to eternity future. That's great news for all of us because it means that He's not going to change the rules on us. We can rely on what the Bible says about Him in the past because He is not going to be different in the future. But how can He be "unchangeable" if our prayers can get Him to change?

We don't know how it works, but this question has been discussed at length by theologians who analyze these things for the rest of us who actually have a life. Some people believe that God never really changed because He knew at the outset how He would respond to our prayers. Some think that there are parts of God's plan that remain a multiple choice until we talk to Him about it—He could go one way or the other depending on how we pray. Other people think that there is no change at all because our prayers fit with what God is going to do anyway (as if God always intended to give Hezekiah 15 more years, but the king needed to pray for it to get in God's plan).

There may be other explanations, but we'll have to think about them after we're finished counting all of the angels on the head of this pin.

Prayer Changes Circumstances. Prayer invokes God's involvement in the circumstances of your life. Yes, that's right, you can get God "on your side" through prayer, and He can really make things happen. But don't take our word for it; look at these true-life examples from the Bible:

✔ Jonah offered a panic prayer as he was getting an "inside view" of the fish's digestive tract. God caused the fish to regurgitate Jonah on the beach (Jonah 2:7-10).

✔ Elijah had a "bed and breakfast" arrangement with a widow in Zarephath. When her son died, Elijah asked God to restore the boy's life. That's exactly what happened (1 Kings 17:8-24). And such incidents weren't limited to the Old Testament. The apostle Peter also prayed over a corpse, and the woman came back to life (Acts 9:36-41).

✔ In what was a cultural disgrace, Hannah couldn't get pregnant. In response to her specific and fervent prayers for a son, she later gave birth to Samuel, whose name means "heard by God" (1 Samuel 1:1-20).

✔ In what must be every weatherman's dream, God caused a drought when Elijah predicted one, and it didn't rain again until years later when Elijah prayed for it (1 Kings 17:1–18:45).

✔ On the night before his trial, Peter was in prison chained between two guards. There was a prayer meeting going on for him in the same town. In the middle of the night, an angel appeared in his cell. The chains fell off, and the angel escorted Peter out of the prison without anybody noticing. (Acts 12:5-11).

GOD IS NOT A LAB RAT

Don't get the idea that you can prove the power of prayer like in a science-fair demonstration. If you had a test group of 100 people praying for a certain situation, you might come up with zilch. That doesn't mean that God doesn't answer prayers. It just means that He doesn't want to be a part of your silly experiment. As we will discuss in Chapter 2, *faith* plays a big part in prayer. If God's actions could be predicted with the laws of probability, then prayer wouldn't require much faith. God chooses when and what He will do, and He wants you to believe in Him for who He is (not because you think He can be reduced to a mathematical equation or a scientific formula).

In your situation, you might be praying for God to:

✔ Get you a new job

✔ Smooth out your relationship problems

✔ Cure a health problem

✔ Fix some problems in your family

✔ Solve your financial problems

These are the kinds of things that God specializes in, but He likes you to talk to Him about them. Don't get the idea that your problem is too big for God to handle, and don't think that He would consider your request to be trivial or insignificant. If it is important to you, then it is important to God. Notice that Jesus didn't put any parameters on the types of requests we could make of God:

Keep on asking, and you will be given what you ask for (Matthew 7:7).

DON'T EXPECT "PRESTO CHANGE-O"

It's true that God answers prayer. But His answer might not always come immediately. And it might not be the answer that you were hoping for. Your timing (usually "ASAP") may not be God's timing. So the change in circumstances may not happen as quickly as you would want it to occur. Also, remember that some of your requests may not happen at all because God knows that what you ask for isn't what's best for you.

God answers prayer. Sometimes His answer is "yes," sometimes it is "later," and sometimes it is "no."

Can You Spare the Change?

Get ready for things to happen when you pray. Prayer changes things. But most of all, be prepared for your prayers to change *you*, because that is the greatest effect of prayer.

✔ *Prayer brings you into God's presence.* Conversing with God takes you out of your humdrum world and connects you with the Creator of the universe. And that happens immediately. God doesn't have a waiting room where you have to sit for 35 minutes before talking with Him. He does not put you on hold and force you to listen to angel harp-plucking (interrupted by an occasional "Thank you for holding; your call is important to God. Please stay on the line, as He answers prayers in the order that they are received"). Nope. When you pray, you are immediately in God's presence.

✔ *Prayer changes your attitude and focus.* Let's admit it. We all tend to be self-centered. Even our prayers can be that way. But as we will discuss in chapter 3, our prayers should properly focus on who God is and what He wants to accomplish in our lives. As we pray sincerely, we begin to align ourselves with God's plans rather than our own. We begin to let go of the death grip we have on our own desires, and we begin to subordinate what we want for His desires. In our prayers, we make God the focal point of our life, so we change from being self-centered to being God-centered.

You'll Be Wasting Your Breath Unless...

Prayer really works—it really changes things—but a lot of prayers fizzle out before they get to the ceiling. There

> *Prayer is an interruption of personal ambition.*
> —Rowland Hogben

are two basic prerequisites for you if your prayers are going to work at all:

Prayer Prerequisite #1: You've got to believe that God exists. If your prayers are going to be effective, you've got to believe in God. This sounds basic, doesn't it? But you would be surprised at how many people who have no belief in God utter some kind of prayer when they have a problem ("just to cover all the bases"). If they don't get out of the trouble immediately, then they use that as further "proof" that God doesn't exist. God is not interested in proving Himself to someone who doesn't even believe that He is real. The Bible explains it this way:

So, you see, it is impossible to please God without faith. Anyone who wants to come to him [God] must believe that there is a God (Hebrews 11:6).

Some people will say that they have *faith* that their prayers will be answered. But that is not the kind of faith that this verse is referring to. It is not belief in getting what you're praying for; it is belief in the God to whom you are praying.

Prayer Prerequisite #2: You've got to have a personal relationship with God. There are many people who believe that God exists (even Satan and the demons believe that). But a belief in God means that you know God. It is possible to have a personal relationship with God (more about that in chapter 2), and prayer is for the people who do. After all, that's what prayer is: you talking to God as a Person you know.

Here is the rest of the last verse that we quoted:

> *Anyone who wants to come to him [God] must believe that there is a God and that he rewards those who sincerely seek him* (Hebrews 11:6).

You are assured of getting in touch with God if you are sincerely seeking Him, but otherwise your prayers may just be a bunch of hot air.

GOD'S GOT "CALLER ID"

Let's clarify something for a minute. Suppose you don't have a personal relationship with God—or maybe you don't even believe that God exists. Either way, God will *still hear* any prayer that you say. He is aware of everything that happens in this world. The Bible says that He knows if a baby sparrow falls out of its nest, so He knows when you are blabbering on about something. But just because He *hears* you, He doesn't have to *listen*. And He certainly is not committed to respond to your prayers.

It is like having caller ID at your home. When the phone rings, you know if a friend or a stranger is calling. If it is your close friend, you are quick to pick up and start chatting away. If it is a stranger, you're likely to let the phone ring unanswered (because you are satisfied with your current long-distance phone service). Well, God is the same way. He is anxious to hear what you have to say if you are His good friend. If you consider Him a stranger, then He is not obligated to pick up. The only exception is when you're calling Him to start a relationship. Then He'll pick up immediately.

"What's That Again?"

1. Don't get caught in a trap of praying for the wrong reasons. You can't expect to be enthusiastic about prayer unless you believe that it really makes a difference.

2. Above everything else, there is one important reason to pray: because God told us to do it.

3. Prayer is part of the process that God uses to work in our lives.

4. Prayer can change a lot of things, but it is most likely to change *you*. Prayer brings *you* into *God's* plan (not the other way around).

Dig Deeper

The Bible is full of examples of prayers that made a difference. If you want to read about circumstances that were changed by prayer, check out:

✔ 2 Kings 20:1-11 (God lets the king live for 15 more years)

✔ 1 Kings 17–18 (in response to Elijah's prayers, God withholds rain for three years and sends fire from heaven at a prophets' face-off)

But the greatest changes made by prayer will happen inside of you:

✔ Read Psalm 40 for King David's auto-biographical description of his inner changes when he started communicating with God.

You might also be interested in reading:

✔ *Praying to the God You Can Trust,* Leith Anderson. The subtitle aptly describes the subject of the book: "Discovering the God of Hope When Prayer Doesn't Seem to Change Things."

✔ *Prayer: The Great Adventure,* David Jeremiah. This is a great book covering the basics of prayer, including the whys and the hows, that lead to the adventure of knowing God.

Moving On

In this chapter we briefly mentioned a few wrong reasons for praying. Saying a prayer for changed circumstances isn't wrong, but you're talking to God with the wrong attitude if you're only doing it for what He can give you. Perhaps the biggest mistake we all make is praying to God for stuff that we want. In the next chapter we'll try to get a perspective on prayer that is something more than "me, me, me."

Chapter 2

GOD ISN'T A WEB SITE: THERE'S MORE TO PRAYER THAN ASKING FOR STUFF

*If we conceive of prayer basically as a
means of acquiring things from God,
we trivialize prayer.*

—Walter Liefeld

BRUCE & STAN SAY It seems as if everyone is on the World Wide Web these days. Why are we so interested in "surfing the Internet"? Basically, it's so we can get stuff: news, information, entertainment, books, music, and useless junk that other people are trying to get rid of.

The Web is an impersonal force, with no personality and no ability to do anything apart from those people who input information and requests. That's exactly how many people view God. He's nothing more than an impersonal force who exists because we input information and requests. They treat God like a Web site, and prayer is like an Internet connection they use to get the stuff they want.

We don't have to tell you (but we will anyway) that God is a whole lot more than a Web site, and prayer is much more than an impersonal connection. Read on and find out for yourself.

Bruce & Stan

Chapter 2

God Isn't a Web Site: There's More to Prayer Than Asking for Stuff

What's Ahead

➤ What prayer isn't
➤ Prayer is talking to God
➤ Who can pray?
➤ Praying in God's will
➤ You can pray for anything

*I*f you've been treating prayer like it's some kind of Internet connection, don't feel bad. We've all been there. We all have to admit that from time to time usually when we're in trouble or we think we need something—we've treated God like some kind of information-highway genie who doesn't do a thing or doesn't give us anything until we rub the magic lamp called prayer.

That's why we think you will agree with us that when it comes to prayer, we need a whole new understanding and a new attitude. We need to see prayer for what it really is, not for what we've made it out to be.

What Prayer Isn't

We've already given you a couple of things that prayer *isn't*. It isn't a Web site (and neither is God) that you click on to get stuff. Neither is prayer a magic lamp that you can activate by saying the right words. Prayer isn't a matter of wishing certain things could happen. Here are some other things prayer isn't:

✔ Prayer isn't a *mystical experience* that you enter into by sitting cross-legged while you chant some inane phrase over and over.

✔ Prayer isn't a *formal experience* practiced by "experts" who wear the proper attire (robes are a favorite), stand on elevated platforms in cold buildings, and pray to God on your behalf (as if they are the only ones who can get God's attention).

✔ Prayer isn't a *formal language* filled with "thous" and "thees" that you have to learn, like some secret code.

✔ Prayer isn't *negotiating with God,* as if you were making some kind of deal: "God, if You do this for me, then I'll do such and such for You."

✔ Prayer isn't an *escape pod* that you climb into only when you're in trouble.

Even though all of us have bought into one or more of these misconceptions about prayer, they don't even begin to tell us what prayer is all about. Prayer is so much simpler, and prayer is so much more.

Prayer Is Talking to God

There are many ways to communicate with someone, but the best and most effective is talking face-to-face in normal, everyday language, with no pretense, no hidden agendas, and no formality.

The same goes for God. Even though you can't see God, it is possible to talk to Him *in person,* and the way you do that is through prayer. In the third century, Clement of Alexandria concluded that prayer is "conversation with God," and we would agree. But we also believe that prayer is much more than conversation, mainly because God is much more than a person. He is God, and above Him there is no other. There is no one in heaven or on earth who can compare. Therefore, conversing with God is something none of us should take for granted. Prayer is an awesome privilege.

"GETTING PERSONAL WITH GOD"

It's really important to understand that God is not an impersonal force. Even though He is invisible, God is personal, and He has all the characteristics of a person: He *knows*, He *hears*, He *feels*, and He *speaks*. We can know this personal God on a personal level because He has intentionally revealed Himself to us through the world, which He created; through the Bible, which He wrote; and through Jesus, whom He sent.

A lot of us tend to think of God as a king sitting on a throne somewhere in heaven. (Hey, don't laugh. That isn't some childhood fantasy. It's a great image of God.) Here's how David—himself a king—envisioned the God that he loved:

> *I lift my eyes to you, O God, enthroned in heaven* (Psalm 123:1).

Okay, so if God is enthroned in heaven, how do we get to Him? Isn't there this huge door between the throne room and us? Yes, there is a door that must be opened, and prayer is the key. Prayer is what gives us access so that we can "come boldly to the throne of our gracious God" (Hebrews 4:16).

Only there's a twist to this story of God as King. The door separating Him and us isn't in His throne room. The door is in our hearts. God doesn't have a door. His throne room is always open. We are the ones who have constructed a barrier between ourselves and the God who made us, who knows us, and who loves us. If our prayers fail to get through to God, it's because our door is closed, not His.

The reason our heart's door is closed is because of sin, which is anything that doesn't meet God's perfect standard (Romans 3:23). The truth is that imperfect people can't come into the presence of a holy God. And if we can't be in His presence, we can't talk to Him.

Many people have this huge misconception that if they simply say, "Hey God, I'm talking to You," they will engage the power of God on their behalf. It's the God-as-genie concept, and it's dead wrong. Yes, prayer does engage the power of God (we'll get to that later in the book), but it doesn't happen when sinful people snap their fingers at God.

Who Can Pray?

So how can anyone pray? Or, as Dr. James Montgomery Boice writes, "How can I, a sinful human being, approach a holy God?" There's only one way. We have to "get right in God's sight" through the Person of Jesus Christ. The Bible is real clear on this, which makes sense, since God is real clear, and the Bible is His message to us.

> *We are made right in God's sight when we*
> *trust in Jesus Christ to take away our sins.*
> *And we all can be saved in this same way,*
> *no matter who we are or what we have*
> *done* (Romans 3:22).

Here's the deal. The way God has chosen
to deal with our sin problem is through
Christ. More specifically, it's through the
death of Jesus Christ. This is what it meant
for God to "give" us His only Son:

> *For God so loved the world that he gave*
> *his only Son, so that everyone who believes*
> *in him will not perish but have eternal life*
> (John 3:16).

Open Your Heart's Door

Jesus has already died for you. Jesus has
already made you "right with God." All
you have to do is receive the free gift of
salvation. And here's how: You open the
door of your heart to Jesus, who is
knocking:

> *Look! Here I stand at the door and knock.*
> *If you hear me calling and open the door, I*
> *will come in, and we will share a meal as*
> *friends* (Revelation 3:20).

You want to get personal with God? Open your heart's door. Do you want to be able to talk to God in a way that will absolutely change your life, both now and forever? Ask Jesus to come into your heart. Do you want to pray with power? Let Jesus lead you into the presence of God.

> *And so, dear brothers and sisters, we can boldly enter heaven's Most Holy Place because of the blood of Jesus. . . . Let us go right into the presence of God* (Hebrews 10:19,22).

THERE'S GOT TO BE ANOTHER WAY

A lot of people have another misconception about God. The way they figure it, there have to be many ways to God, and therefore many ways to talk to God. Don't believe it. There's only one way, and it's through the Person of Jesus Christ. Hey, don't take our word for it. Here's what Jesus said:

> *I am the way, the truth, and the life. No one can come to the Father except through me (John 14:6).*

You could look all your life and never find another way to God. You could pray all your life to a god of your own choosing and never know what it's like to have direct access to God through Jesus Christ.

Can You Ever Close the Door?

Knowing that you are "right with God" through Jesus Christ is the greatest thing in the world. Not only is your eternal life in heaven secure, but your life here on earth also takes on new meaning and power—a power that is unleashed through prayer.

In chapter 4, we're going to talk about how to pray with purpose and power, but before we get to that, we have some unfinished business in this area of sin (sorry, it just keeps coming up).

Make no mistake about it. When you believe by faith that God saves you because of what Jesus has already done for you (Romans 5:1), you are saved—forever. Nothing and no one can separate you from the awesome power of God's love (Romans 8:38).

But you are still an imperfect person— made right in God's sight, but still imperfect. The apostle Paul called it a "fact of life" for the believer. See if you can identify with what Paul writes: "When I want to do what is right, I inevitably do what is wrong" (Romans 7:21). Don't you hate when that happens? So does God. He loves you, but He hates your sin.

When you hold on to some sin, God won't let you into His presence. He can't (remember, He's holy). In effect, you shut the door to your heart, and God won't listen to a thing you say to Him. The prophet Isaiah put it this way:

Listen! The LORD is not too weak to save you, and he is not becoming deaf. He can hear you when you call. But there is a problem—your sins have cut you off from God. Because of your sin, he has turned away and will not listen anymore (Isaiah 59:1-2).

Please understand what the Bible says. God has saved you. God can hear you when you pray. But when you sin, God won't listen.

BUT I DON'T FEEL SAVED

Besides stifling your prayers, sin has another consequence. Whenever we neglect the sin in our lives, we move away from God and can even get to the point where we don't feel saved. R. C. Sproul writes: "Although a true Christian cannot lose his salvation, he can lose his assurance of salvation." Even if we've felt close to God for years, the joy of our salvation can disappear if we allow sin to continue.

Confession and Forgiveness

Okay, we kind of tricked you here. It isn't exactly true that God won't listen to your prayers when you sin. There is one prayer He will hear: your prayer of confession.

Confession is such a "churchy" word. It may bring up some painful memories for you. You might equate confession with a secret procedure involving little rooms and third parties. Forget that stuff. Confession is something personal between you and God. And it's absolutely necessary if you want to keep the communication channel from you to God open.

When you admit to God that you have sinned, here's what's going to happen:

But if we confess our sins to him, he is faithful and just to forgive us and to cleanse us from every wrong (1 John 1:9).

Confession isn't just good for the soul; it opens your heart's door so that you can once again come into the presence of God.

> *If I had not confessed the sin in my heart, my Lord would not have listened. But God did listen! He paid attention to my prayer. Praise God, who did not ignore my prayer and did not withdraw his unfailing love from me* (Psalm 66:18-20).

Praying in God's Will

There are really only two conditions for prayer. We have already talked about the first, and here's the second: *God wants us to pray according to His will.*

> *And we can be confident that he will listen to us whenever we ask him for anything in line with his will* (1 John 5:14).

Even Jesus prayed to His Father with this condition in place: "Yet I want your will, not mine" (Matthew 26:39).

We admit, this doesn't sound like a walk in the park. How are we supposed to know what God's will is when we pray? We could write an entire book on God's will (hey, not a bad idea), but right now we want to suggest two things we think will help you pray in God's will:

1. *Pray the Bible.* Our good friends David and Heather Kopp have written a series of books called *Praying the Bible.* The books cover important subjects like your life and your family. The idea is that since the Bible is God's Word for us, it is also His will for us. Praying the Bible involves "digging into God's Word to discover the Lord's deepest desires for His people, and praying these promises, claims, and truths back to Him." Therefore, the first step to knowing God's will is to know His Word.

2. *Pray with Faith.* The Bible is God's inspired message to us, "and is useful to teach us what is true and to make us realize what is wrong in our lives" (2 Timothy 3:16). But what about those times when the Bible

> We should have great confidence that God will answer our prayer when we ask him for something that accords with a specific promise or command of Scripture.
>
> ——Wayne Grudem

doesn't have a specific answer to what we are praying for? This is when we have to pray with faith. We need to trust God to have our best interest in mind at all times. We need to have "the confident assurance that what we hope for is going to happen" (Hebrews 11:1).

Prayer and Desire

When you meet the two conditions of prayer—

✔ your heart's door is completely open

✔ you are praying in God's will

something wonderful happens. The desires of your heart match up with God's desires. You literally become a person with a heart for God. This is the place where God wants you. This is where He can use you. To have a heart for God means that you are tuned to His frequency. The communication channel between you and God is crystal-clear. When you pray, God listens. When He speaks, you can hear Him.

You don't have to be perfect to have a heart for God. The Bible says that King

David—despite his rather huge failings and weaknesses—was a man after God's own heart. That's why David was able to write:

Take delight in the LORD, and he will give you your heart's desires (Psalm 37:4).

Can you imagine being so connected to God that you delight in Him? As you pray, the desires of your heart will match up with God's desires. Your prayer life will be filled with purpose, power, and passion (more about that in chapter 4).

You Can Pray for Anything

Some people are puzzled by something Jesus said about prayer.

Listen to me! You can pray for anything, and if you believe, you will have it (Mark 11:24).

Maybe this is how some people get the idea that God is a

> *Prayer is no fitful, short-lived thing. It is no voice crying unheard and unheeded in the silence. It is a voice that goes into God's ear.*
> —E.M. Bounds

genie, obligated to give us stuff just because we ask. Certainly that's not what Jesus meant. Jesus was directly referring to faith as the "confident assurance that what we hope for is going to happen" (Hebrews 11:1).

You don't believe by *wishing*. You believe by *trusting* God, who knows you and your situation better than anyone. God doesn't grant wishes. He answers all the prayers of people who have a heart for Him. If our desires match God's desires, then we will receive what we pray for. The key is to keep our heart's door open and to pray in God's will.

"What's That Again?"

1. Prayer isn't a mystical experience, a formal experience, or a formal language. Prayer isn't negotiating with God, and it isn't an escape pod.

2. Prayer is simply talking to a personal God, who loves you and knows you and knows what's best for you.

3. The first condition of prayer is for you to "get right with God" through Jesus Christ. This opens your heart to God. And you keep the door of your heart open to God by asking Him to forgive your sins after you goof up.

4. The second condition of prayer is to pray in God's will.

5. You can pray for anything if you have a heart for God and believe that He will answer.

Dig Deeper

Is this stuff starting to make sense? We wish we could spend more time going deeper into these incredible truths about prayer, but since this is a pocket guide, our greatest hope is to get you thinking—and praying.

If you want to learn more about what it means to have a heart for God, read the Psalms, most of which were written by David. Or you may want to read the story of David in a book. Our personal favorite is called *David: A Man of Passion and Destiny* by Charles Swindoll. And if you want a great book on knowing God's will, read another gem by Swindoll, *The Mystery of God's Will: What Does He Want for Me?*

Finally, here are some additional classic books on prayer:

- *All Things Are Possible Through Prayer*, Charles L. Allen. Practical and easy-to-read, filled with true stories about the effects of prayer.

- *How to Pray*, R. A. Torrey. A true classic, and only 100 pages long. Dr. Torrey lists 11 reasons why prayer is important.

- *E. M. Bounds on Prayer*, E. M. Bounds. This one-volume collection includes seven books by the man who has written more about prayer than anyone else (well, except for God). This is a must for your personal library.

Moving On

John Calvin (the French theologian, not the friend of Hobbes) saw prayer as "digging up" God's treasures. He wasn't referring to earthly stuff. He was talking about the treasures of "grace and glory" that are available to us in Jesus Christ. Since Jesus made it possible for us to come into the presence of God through prayer, shouldn't we learn more about how Jesus prayed and what He taught about prayer? Hey, it makes sense to us, so that's where we're going next.

We'll also look at what it means to pray in Jesus' name, and we'll discover that Jesus is still very much involved in our prayers.

Chapter 3

WHAT TO SAY WHEN YOU PRAY: DO WORDS REALLY MATTER?

I may use the most beautiful words and phrases, but until I am connected with the Great Source of power, my prayers are just meaningless words.

—Charles L. Allen

Well, we've talked about why to pray in chapter 1 (because God said to do it and because it works). And in chapter 2 we discussed that prayer is simply talking to God, beginning with getting right with Him and then getting aligned with His will. So maybe now you're ready to actually start praying.

But wait!

- What are you going to say? You can ask for stuff, but should you start off with that? Maybe it would be better to start off with a few thanksgiving-type phrases. Are there subjects you should avoid, like politics or sex?

- And how are you going to say it? Do you have to sound like the King James version of the Bible?

- And should you be standing or sitting . . . or maybe even kneeling (that seems like a religious thing, too).

These are honest questions, and we've got a great place to go for the answers. Let's see how Jesus prayed, and we can copy that.

Bruce & Stan

Chapter 3

What to Say When You Pray: Do Words Really Matter?

here are a few occasions when you are speechless and don't know what to say. Maybe you try to say something—you even open your mouth and move your jaw—but nothing comes out. It seems to happen to everyone when:

✔ You split the seam in the seat of your pants on the playground in the fourth grade.

✔ The highway patrol officer asks if you know how fast you were driving.

✔ You open your wallet at the cashier in the restaurant and see nothing but lint.

And, number one on everyone's speechless list would be "Trying to talk to God for the first time."

But don't freak out if you've tried praying and the only noises that came out of your mouth were guttural grunts that sounded like you had a clogged trachea. It really isn't that hard once you know what to pray about and what to say. As a matter of fact, it's as easy as . . . talking.

Jesus Knew What He Was Talking About

Jesus understood that all of us would have difficulty talking to God unless we knew what we were supposed to say. To help us out, He gave a sample prayer to His disciples in Matthew 6:9-13. You might recognize it best in the old-fashioned King James version of the Bible:

After this manner therefore pray ye: Our Father which art in heaven, hallowed be thy name. Thy kingdom come. Thy will be done in earth, as it is in heaven. Give us this day our daily bread. And forgive us our debts, as we forgive our debtors. And lead us not into temptation, but deliver us from evil: For thine is the kingdom, and the power, and the glory, for ever. Amen.

This sample prayer is usually referred to as "the Lord's Prayer." You can find it printed on laminated wall plaques, on bookmarks, and sometimes written on the backside of a postage stamp (usually by some calligrapher who has a magnifying glass and strained eyesight).

We thought it would be helpful to study the components of the Lord's Prayer. After all, it was the pattern that Jesus told us to follow. But as poetic as the King James version sounds, we think it will be helpful if we study the Lord's Prayer in a more modern version. Here is how it reads in the New Living Translation:

Pray like this: Our Father in heaven, may your name be honored. May your Kingdom come soon. May your will be done here on earth, just as it is in heaven. Give us our food for today, and forgive us our sins, just as we have forgiven those who have sinned against us. And don't let us yield to temptation, but deliver us from the evil one. For yours is the kingdom and the power and the glory forever. Amen.

Following the Pattern

Let's dissect this prayer and see what we can learn about how we should talk to God:

- *Our Father:* It is always good to start off our prayer reminding ourselves of our personal relationship to God. He is our heavenly Father, and He loves us because we are His own spiritual children.

- *In heaven:* We need to remind ourselves of God's majesty, that He is in control of the universe, and that nothing is too difficult for Him.

- *May your name be honored:* We shouldn't be hollering at God like we would at a peanut vendor at a baseball game. He is worthy of our respect and

devotion. Our praise to Him is appropriate because of who He is, and it
keeps us in the right frame of mind.

- *May your Kingdom come soon:* Christ is
going to come back to earth someday,
and He will rule over it. Remembering
this fact will chisel some of the arro-
gance out of our lives.

- *May your will be done here on earth,
just as it is in heaven:* We need to adopt
God's priorities as our own. He needs to
be the primary influence in our personal
life, in our family life, on the job, and in
whatever we do.

- *Give us our food for today:* God wants
us to be asking Him for the things that
we need and want. (If we are praying in
His will, then we'll be asking for the
things He might already want us to
have.)

- *And forgive us our sins:* In chapter 2, we
talked about keeping the door of our
heart open to God by confessing our
sins. Sin interrupts the conversation we
can have with Him, so it is important to

always keep the line of communication free from "sin static."

- *Just as we have forgiven those who have sinned against us:* Wait a minute—this is getting too personal! But hey, we're talking to a very personal God. He wants us to be praying about our relationships and how we treat other people.

- *And don't let us yield to temptation, but deliver us from the evil one:* We should pray that God will help us overcome (and avoid) those circumstances that tempt us to sin. We live at the center of spiritual warfare, and we want God on our side.

- *For yours is the kingdom and the power and the glory forever:* The prayer ends the same way that it begins—praising God. Isn't it amazing that God cares for us and that He wants us talking to Him? Don't forget to tell Him that you appreciate it.

SHOULD YOU SAY "AMEN" EVEN IF YOU AREN'T A BAPTIST?

There is nothing magic about the word *amen*. It means "let it be so." It is a traditional "sign off" for prayers, but it is not required. You could just say, "Over and out," and God wouldn't be offended.

Look at the different categories that this one prayer covers:

✔ Praise (acknowledging God's importance in our lives)

✔ Priorities (wanting His will instead of our own)

✔ Provision (asking for what we need)

✔ Personal relationships (talking about how we relate with other people)

✔ Protection (asking for help to live a godly and moral life)

Your prayers don't have to be any different or any more complicated. Just talk to God about these kinds of things.

CAN YOU SIMPLIFY IT A BIT?

Since Jesus gave the Lord's Prayer as a model, that is a good example for us to follow. But all of the components of the Lord's Prayer may be a little too much to remember at first. We like the way that the elements of prayer have been summarized by James Montgomery Boice with the acronym "ACTS."

A: Adoration   Praising God for how great He is.

C: Confession   Telling God that we are sorry for the wrong things that we have done.

T: Thanksgiving   Expressing our gratitude to God for all of the good things He has given to us and done for us.

S: Supplication   Asking God to work in the circumstances of our lives and asking for His involvement in the lives of other people.

Personally, we think *supplication* is too much of a "churchy" word for common usage, but it is accurate and it makes for a nice acronym.

Does God require "Thee" and "Thou" references? Now we know *what* to talk about, but let's discuss *how* we should say it.

> What language does God speak?
> Does He prefer formality?
> Or can we be casual?

Here are the answers: "All of them"; "Not unless we prefer it"; and "Yes." Do you get the point? God has been listening to prayers for thousands of years. During that time, people have been praying in a lot of different languages and a lot of different styles. They have prayed while they are mad and happy and scared and thoughtful (although not usually with all of those emotions at the same time). God wants us to pray the way we feel.

Sounds like . . . Have you ever heard your voice played back on a tape recorder? It sounds weird, doesn't it? Do you worry about how your voice should sound when you pray to God? Well, don't. God doesn't care if you speak with a Shakespearean accent or with a Southern drawl. He doesn't even care if your words are audible. He can hear what you are thinking in your head, so you've got your choice:

Option 1: Pray silently to yourself in your mind.

Option 2: Talk to God out loud.

Option 3: Pray silently, but with your lips still moving (you know, like some people do when they are reading).

WHAT TIME IS THE RIGHT TIME?

Daniel (you know, the guy in the lions' den) used to pray at set intervals during the day. King David (of Goliath and slingshot fame) had a habit of praying early in the morning. Does this mean that God prefers you to pray at a fixed time?

Don't worry about when to pray. God doesn't have to schedule you for a time slot in His planner to avoid conflicts with prayer times for the rest of the world's population. (God's appointment book doesn't read anything like: "M/W/F 10:07–10:22 A.M., talking with Sarah from Pasadena.") Anytime is a great time to talk with God. After all, the Bible says that we should be praying all the time (Ephesians 6:18).

Having a regular prayer time will probably help you so that your time with God doesn't get lost in the shuffle of your busy day. But just in case you were wondering, here are some examples of when your prayers might be spontaneous:

• If you're caught driving in a snowstorm, you'll want to pray for safety. (And we suggest praying with your eyes open.)

• When you are at school and the teacher springs a pop quiz on you, you'll be praying. (Don't pray for an "A" because God may not feel like performing a miracle. Maybe you should just pray that God brings back to your memory all of the facts that you studied.)

• When you are at that family reunion, pray that God will give you patience with your irritating relatives. Say an extra prayer if you feel an urge to smash the rhubarb pie in Aunt Carol's face.

• You can pray that God will help you resist temptation if you find yourself at a place where you shouldn't be or with people who are doing things that you shouldn't do. (This prayer is most effective if you say it while you are turning around and walking in the opposite direction.)

- As you drive through the mountains and see a magnificent view, talk to God and thank Him for creating such a beautiful world. (You can say the same prayer when you are enjoying the splendor of the ocean. Actually, you could probably do that same thing anywhere in the world, except maybe Fresno.)

Anytime is the right time to pray. In fact, anytime is the best time to pray.

Putting Words in Your Mouth

What if you want to pray about a situation but don't know what to ask for? What if you are going through a difficult time and just can't explain it? Maybe you are so sad or emotionally distraught that you can't articulate your feelings. What if you want to pray for God's will, but don't know what it is?

God has got these situations covered, too. Everyone who has a personal relationship with God has the Holy Spirit alive within them. One of the jobs of the Holy Spirit is to pray on our behalf when we don't know what to say:

And the Holy Spirit helps us in our distress. For we don't even know what we should pray for, nor how we should pray. But the Holy Spirit prays for us with groanings that cannot be expressed in words. And the Father who knows all hearts knows what the Spirit is saying, for the Spirit pleads for us believers in harmony with God's own will (Romans 8:26-27).

If you find yourself in this situation, just hang in there. Tell God that you don't know how you should be praying, so you're letting the Holy Spirit do it for you.

HOW MUCH IS ENOUGH?

Do all of our prayers have to be as long as a presidential campaign speech? (Most of us aren't as long-winded as politicians. Except Bruce. He's a lawyer and gets paid by the minute, so he can really stretch things out.) Can some of our prayers be meaningful if they are short? (Hey, the Gettysburg Address was written on the back of an envelope.) Will God be offended if we only have a few words to say and then want to end it?

God cares more about *what* you say than how long it takes to spit it out. Short prayers are

> sometimes the most effective ones. In some situations, you won't have the luxury of time for a lengthy prayer (like when the rip cord gets stuck and your parachute won't open).
>
> God listens to unspoken, instantaneous prayers. When King Cyrus asked a question and expected an immediate response, Nehemiah said a mental split-second prayer before he answered the king. God heard and answered the prayer (check it out at Nehemiah 2:1-8).

Shut Up and Listen

Notice that we have referred to prayer as talking *with* God—not talking *to* God. Prayer is a two-way conversation. We do some of the talking while God listens. But then we need to let God do some of the talking while we listen.

At this point you might be thinking that Bruce and Stan have lost the few shreds of sanity that they had. Well, let us explain. When we refer to letting God talk, we don't expect that you will be hearing little angel voices in your head. We don't even think that you will hear James Earl Jones speaking in his Darth Vader voice from the heavens. God doesn't usually talk that way anymore.

God is most likely to speak to you in the quietness of your thoughts. As you pray in His will, you are going to get a sense of what He wants. He will speak to you by prompting your thoughts.

In your prayer time, you should leave time for God to talk to you. Let Him have His turn. God has even said that you should shut up for a while and listen for Him (only He said it a little more tactfully):

> *Be silent, and know that I am God* (Psalm 46:10).

GOING PUBLIC

Most of the time you will be praying by yourself, but it doesn't always have to be that way. People can pray together in groups. It usually works like this: One person starts by praying out loud, and when that person is finished, the next person goes for a while. Maybe they have agreed in advance over who will pray for what. Don't worry if your style doesn't sound as good as someone else's. It's not a contest, and God won't be holding up a little scorecard like a judge at a skating competition.

Name That Prayer

As you read verses in the New Testament about prayer, you'll see a lot of references to praying "in Jesus' name." Here's a famous one that Jesus said Himself:

> *You can ask for anything in my name, and I will do it. . . . Yes, ask anything in my name, and I will do it!* (John 14:13-14).

Two things occur to us from reading this quote. First, Jesus must have really wanted us to get the idea since He repeated Himself. And secondly, we really like the idea of getting whatever we ask for.

Praying in the name of Jesus doesn't mean we have to keep repeating the phrase "in Jesus' name" during our prayer. It is not a magical formula that makes wishes come true. Rather, praying in Jesus' name means that we are praying with the authority that He gives to us as children of God because He paid the penalty for our sins. Praying in His name also means that we are praying in His will for the things that He wants, not for the things that we want. (And this means that prayer doesn't give us whatever we ask for out of selfishness, just whatever we ask for within the parameters of His will.)

JESUS TALKS TO GOD ABOUT REAL LIFE

The Lord's Prayer was an example that Jesus gave to His disciples when He was teaching them about prayer. But the Bible doesn't indicate that He ever used that same prayer when He was praying on His own. Are you interested in how Jesus talked to God in His own prayers? Chapter 17 of the Gospel of John records what Jesus said to God on the night before the crucifixion. There was some straight talking going on there as Jesus prayed for His friends (His disciples). Another prayer from that same night is found in Luke 22:39-44, when Jesus said that He would prefer to avoid the torture of the crucifixion, but said that He was willing to go along with God's plan no matter what:

Father, if you are willing, please take this cup of suffering away from me. Yet I want your will, not mine (Luke 22:42).

Don't be afraid to be totally honest in your prayers. Jesus was in His.

Praying with Body Language

By this point in the chapter, maybe you feel a little more confident about what your mouth should be saying during your prayers. But what about the rest of your body? If you went to Sunday school when you were a little kid, maybe you feel compelled to close your eyes and fold your hands. Well, that's not mandatory (it was only to keep you from looking around and to keep your finger out of your nose). Actually, the Bible describes people praying in a variety of positions.

- **Pick a Prayer Posture:**

    ✔ *Standing:* In many cultures it is customary to stand in the presence of royalty. Standing during your prayer time can remind you of the respect that God deserves.

    ✔ *Sitting:* If you're reading your Bible at your desk, God will be mighty glad if you start praying right there.

✔ *Kneeling:* This position acknowledges our humility in God's presence.

✔ *Lying on your back:* Psalm 63:6 mentions praying while lying awake in bed. It is certainly comfortable, but you might find the "lying awake" part to be difficult if you don't start until after Letterman or Leno.

✔ *Lying facedown on the ground:* In the cultures during Bible times, this was a position of repentance. Personally, it is not our favorite prayer position (because we find it a little hard on the nose).

- **Give God a Hand**

   ✔ *Hands folded:* Many people prefer to pray this way, and you see it in a lot of religious pictures.

   ✔ *Hands raised:* This is a posture of surrender or of worship. It is usually done with the palms up (otherwise, if you used only one arm with the palm facing outward, it would look like a Hitler salute).

> ✔ *Hands in your pockets:* We see this a lot at church when people are standing in prayer. Actually, this is never mentioned in the Bible, but that is because the Bible was written before pants were invented.

- **The Eyes Have It**

    > ✔ *Eyes Closed:* There is nothing particularly religious or holy about closing your eyes. It just helps you keep your thoughts focused on God.

    > ✔ *Eyes Open:* This is the preferred way if you happen to be praying while you're driving.

We hope you get the point here. There is no "right" or "wrong" posture for prayer. God is more interested in the attitude of your heart than the position of your body. Experiment a little bit so you don't get in a prayer rut.

"What's That Again?"

1. The Lord's Prayer is a good pattern for us to follow, but we don't need to copy it verbatim. Our prayers should include elements of praising God, thanking God, and asking God.

2. There is no one correct style for praying. Just be yourself and talk with God about what is on your heart.

3. Prayer is a two-way conversation with God. Give Him a chance to talk to you, and this means you'll need to sit still for a moment and listen.

4. There are lots of different ways to pray: privately or in a group, kneeling or sitting or standing, out loud or silently. They are all acceptable. God is more concerned about the condition of your heart than the position of your body.

Dig Deeper

You don't have to be an experienced artist to do something artistic. (Just look at the refrigerator door of any mother with a preschooler.) With a little practice, your artistic skills can improve. Well, praying is an art form, too. And here are a few books that can give you some excellent pointers as you practice talking to God.

- *A Life of Prayer,* Paul Cedar. This book starts with the request the disciples asked of Jesus: "Lord, teach us to pray." It gives insightful suggestions and instructions.

- *Too Busy Not to Pray,* Bill Hybels. This book starts with a great title and gets better after that. Written by the pastor of America's largest church, it will help you find time to pray.

- *Let Prayer Change Your Life,* Becky Tirabassi. Ms. Tirabassi conducts group workshops on prayer. This book contains some practical pointers about keeping a prayer notebook.

Moving On

When you start praying for the first time, it will seem both awkward and awesome. After a while it will become more comfortable for you. But if you are like many people, after a longer while prayer becomes a little routine. It even seems to be a little boring. The newness wears off after a while, and you fall into a prayer rut. Nobody likes prayer when you get to that stage—especially God.

But prayer wasn't designed by God to be that way. He wants your prayers to be dynamic and exciting. He wants you to really enjoy talking with Him. He wants prayer to be the highlight of your day. We guess that you want the same thing. If so, keep reading, because in chapter 4 we'll be talking about how you can energize your prayers.

Chapter 4

PUMPED-UP PRAYER: TALKING TO GOD WITH POWER, PURPOSE, AND PASSION

> *In these days we have sore need of a generation of praying people, a band of men and women through whom God can bring His greatest movements more fully into the world.*
>
> —E. M. Bounds

Do you sometimes feel like a spiritual weakling? Then we have a fitness program for you: *Pump up your prayer life!* Just like exercise increases your physical stamina and overall health, prayer will do wonders for your overall spiritual life.

Like spiritual versions of Hans and Frans (but without the padding), we want to (*clap*) pump you up by sharing how you can pray with power, purpose, and passion.

Bruce & Stan

Chapter 4

Pumped-Up Prayer: Talking to God with Power, Purpose, and Passion

* *

What's Ahead

➤ Praying with power
➤ Praying with purpose
➤ Praying with passion
➤ Praying with persistence and patience

*M*ay the force be with you." How many times have you heard that? It probably depends on how many times you've seen *Star Wars*. When you think about it, the idea of some all-powerful "force" in the world is pretty far-fetched. Or is it? Forget George Lucas for a minute. Get the image of Obi-Wan Kenobi out of your head (it's about time). Instead, think about what you've been reading in this little pocket guide. Think about prayer.

What is prayer, but a force? E. M. Bounds, who has written more about prayer than anyone, called prayer "the force that shapes the world." He wrote:

> *The prayers of God's saints are the capital stock in heaven by which Christ carries on His great work upon the earth. Great throes and mighty convulsions in the world have come about as a result of these prayers. The earth is changed, revolutionized; angels move on more powerful, more rapid wings; and God's policy is shaped when the prayers of His people are more numerous and more efficient.*

Do you believe that? Do you believe your prayers have the potential of moving the hand of God? You better believe it! Prayer is more than you or we or George Lucas could ever imagine. Prayer is the greatest force in the world, and it's real.

Praying with Power

It must have been such a kick to walk around with Jesus. He was always coming up with wild stuff like this that must have left His disciples speechless:

Have faith in God. I assure you that you can say to this mountain, "May God lift you up and throw you into the sea," and your command will be obeyed. All that's required is that you really believe and do not doubt in your heart (Mark 11:22-23).

The Bible doesn't say how Jesus' followers responded to His statement about moving mountains through prayer, but they must have been a little skeptical. Aren't you?

Mountain-Moving Prayer

Did Jesus really mean you could literally move a mountain just by praying? Of course not. Jesus was fond of using figurative language to drive home a point. His point here is that moving a mountain would appear to be an impossible task. Yet that's exactly what God is capable of doing—the impossible.

Do you have an impossible task facing you right now? God can handle it. Is there something overwhelming in your future? Give it to God. When you get to the point where human effort has no effect, that's where God can work. For future reference, memorize these words from Jesus:

Humanly speaking, it is impossible. But with God everything is possible (Matthew 19:26).

When you truly believe that God can do the impossible, pray with an open heart in God's will, and God will answer. That's mountain-moving prayer.

Praying with Faith

Bill Hybels gives two principles for building and praying with a faith that moves mountains:

✔ *Faith comes from looking at God, not at the mountain.* When an impossible situation faces you, it's tempting to look at the mountain. We become like Peter when he was walking on the water (Matthew 14:25-32). He was doing fine as long as he kept his eyes on Jesus, but as soon as he looked around and focused on the waves, he began to sink. When you pray, keep your eyes on the Lord, not on the storm.

✔ *God gives us faith as we walk with Him.* Your faith is like a muscle. If you don't exercise it, your faith grows weak. But if you use it every day, your faith will grow strong because God will add to it.

Praying with Purpose

As your faith muscle grows, the force of your prayer will grow stronger as well. You'll find yourself becoming a prayer superhero! Actually, the traditional description is more like a prayer *warrior*. History is filled with the stories of faithful saints who prayed tirelessly for God to move in the lives of individuals, neighborhoods, nations, and the world. It's likely that a prayer warrior has prayed for you, whether you know it or not!

You really don't have to be a superhero to be a prayer warrior. Any ordinary person will do. You just have to be faithful to God and His

How do you pray a prayer so filled with faith that it can move a mountain? By shifting the focus from the size of your mountain to the sufficiency of the mountain mover, and by stepping forward in obedience. As you walk with God, your faith will grow, your confidence will increase and your prayer will have power.

—Bill Hybels

Word. God desires to do mighty things in you, your neighborhood, your nation, and your world. But He needs you to pray! E. M. Bounds wrote:

> *Men and women are needed whose prayers will give to the world the utmost power of God, whose prayers will make His promises blossom with rich and full results. God is waiting to hear us, and He challenges us to pray that He might work.*

Seven Things You Can Pray For

If you want to pray with purpose, you need to be deliberate and specific. Here are some suggestions:

Pray for others. "People must pray, and people must be prayed for," wrote Bounds. You can pray for anything you want, but people should be at the top of your list. Pray for people who are hurting, people who are confused, people who are lonely, and people who don't think they need God. Ask God to give you a heart for people. There's no place for a "loner" in the body of Christ. And when you pray for people, don't pray in general terms, like the classic, "Lord, we pray for all the missionaries in the foreign fields." When you pray with purpose, you pray for people by name.

Pray for the lost. Do you sometimes get frustrated with the way people openly reject Jesus? Pray! Our hearts should break over people whose eternal destinies are without hope. We have the answer, and we need to tell others. But before we can say a thing, we need to pray. Evelyn Christenson writes: "In pre-evangelism praying, we ask the omnipotent God of the universe to reach down and work in people's lives *before* we do. And what a difference such praying makes!"

THE PRAYER WARRIOR AND SPIRITUAL WARFARE

Praying for the lost is serious business, because it puts you right into the middle of the great cosmic struggle between good and evil, and between God and Satan. This is where true spiritual warfare happens:

> *For we are not fighting against people made of flesh and blood, but against the evil rulers and authorities of the unseen world, against those mighty powers of darkness who rule this world, and against wicked spirits in the heavenly realms* (Ephesians 6:12).

Don't think for a minute that the struggle between God and Satan is a fair fight. It's not even close! God and Satan are not opposites. Satan cannot and will not win, but he is our enemy (1 Peter 5:8). We can't fight him on our own. We need to engage the power of God through purposeful prayer, so that God will work in the hearts of those we are praying for.

Pray for healing. Medical science has made tremendous advancements in health and disease control. Today our life expectancy is twice what it was 100 years ago. Yet sickness is everywhere, from temporary ailments to illnesses for which there are no cures.

Whether you are sick or someone you know is suffering, your first response should be to pray with purpose and faith, for God is the God who heals (Exodus 15:26). Charles Allen lists these four steps to gain healing and health through faith and prayer:

1. Believe that God can and will heal.

2. Believe that God can use medical science to accomplish His purposes.

3. Remove all "spiritual hindrances" to healing, such as sin and wrong attitudes.

4. Accept God's will for our lives.

Pray for peace of mind. Is there anything more desirable in the world than peace of mind? Everyone wants it, yet few people know how to get it. Hey, it's not as complicated as people think. Our experience has been that the surest way to peace of mind is through prayer.

> You will keep in perfect peace all who trust in you, whose thoughts are fixed on you! (Isaiah 26:3).

We worry about so many things, and yet there is only one thing we can do for peace of mind. We need to pray and believe that God will supply all our needs and ease our mind.

Trust in the LORD with all your heart; do not depend on your own understanding. Seek his will in all you do, and he will direct your paths (Proverbs 3:5,6).

Pray for confidence in the future. We seem to worry most about the future, don't we? What's going to happen? What will we do? How will we ever get through such and such? Where will we go? What if . . . ? The future can be a scary place, and there's only one thing you can do to gain confidence for what lies ahead: Pray to the God who knows the future.

Someone once said, "I don't know what the future holds, but I know who holds the future." That's a powerful statement. We can have confidence in the future because we can have confidence in God. Don't pray to *know* what the future holds (God won't tell you anyway), but pray for the confidence to handle whatever happens. God doesn't promise to take away potential problems, but He will equip you to handle them.

Pray for repentance. The first step in giving your life to Christ is repentance. To repent means "to go in the opposite direction." God saves by His grace (Ephesians 2:8,9), but you must willingly turn your back on sin. As we discussed in chapter 2, once God saves you, He saves you. But you still have the capacity to sin. All Christians do. That's why we need to keep walking away from sin. We still need to repent.

A key part of praying with purpose is praying for repentance—for yourself and for your fellow be-lievers. Sin will drag us down; repentance puts us back in line with God's agenda. Evelyn Christenson writes that repentance involves several steps. First, we must admit that our wrongdoings are sin (as opposed to mistakes and errors in judg-ment). Second, we need to recognize that our sins offend a holy God; we can't take them lightly. Third, we must

BIG IDEA

> ### The Discipline of Prayer
> *Like everything else in your spiritual life, prayer doesn't just happen. It takes dis-cipline. Many prayer experts suggest that you keep a daily journal in which you record your prayer requests and an-swers. At the very least, write down some things you want to talk to God about before you pray.*

confess our sins to God in prayer and ask for forgiveness. The final step involves turning away from our sin. Every step involves prayer.

Pray for revival. An amazing thing happens when God's people pray and seek the Lord and turn away from sin. Read it for yourself:

Then if my people who are called by my name will humble themselves and pray and seek my face and turn from their wicked ways, I will hear from heaven and will forgive their sins and heal their land (2 Chronicles 7:14).

God promises to "heal the land" where His people live. So many times we blame our leaders or the culture for the negative things going on in our nation. We believe that conditions in the world will get better only if people without the Lord turn to Him. Yes, we should pray for that to happen. But even more importantly, we need to pray that God's people will turn back to God. Read that verse again. It's the prayers of God's people that move God to heal our land, not the prayers of pagans. And when God's people pray with purpose, revival comes.

Praying with Passion

When we pray with *power,* we believe that God will do the impossible. When we pray with *purpose,* we get very specific in who and what we pray for. But there's another step that's essential if we want our prayers to be effective. We need to learn to pray with *passion.*

When you are passionate about someone or something, there are very strong feelings involved. You get emotional. That's the way you need to approach your prayer life. Put some feeling into it! Don't just give God lip service. Pour your heart into your prayers. ·

THE PASSION OF JESUS

There was no one more passionate about praying than Jesus. In chapter 3 we asked you to read John 17 and Luke 22:39-44, where Jesus prayed for His disciples the night before His crucifixion. Take a closer look at *how* Jesus prayed: "He prayed more fervently, and he was in such agony of spirit that his sweat fell to the ground like great drops of blood" (Luke 22:44). Talk about passion! Jesus poured His emotions, His body, and His heart into his prayers. We may not sweat blood when we pray, but we definitely need to sweat!

Intercessory Prayer

You will be most passionate when you pray for other people. The theological term for this is *intercession.* Here's what it means. When you pray for other people, you literally plead to God on their behalf. That's what it means to intercede. The Bible is full of people who pleaded to God on behalf of others.

✔ Abraham interceded on behalf of his nephew Lot, and God listened (Genesis 18:16-33).

✔ Moses prayed to God on behalf of the people of Israel (this happened often), and God heard him (Numbers 11:1,2).

✔ Elijah pleaded with God to prove Himself to the people of Israel and

the pagan prophets, and God
answered (1 Kings 18:36,37).

And here's the real kicker. Jesus is interceding for us right now!

Who then will condemn us? Will Christ
Jesus? No, for he is the one who died
for us and was raised to life for us and
is sitting at the place of highest honor
next to God, pleading for us (Romans
8:34).

Isn't that incredible? The Son of God, our
Savior, didn't pray to God just when He
was on the earth. He is praying—He is
pleading—to God right now, and He's
doing it for us. This should humble us and
motivate us to pray for other people, regardless of who they are.

I urge you, first of all, to pray for all
people. As you make your requests, plead
for God's mercy upon them, and give
thanks (1 Timothy 2:1).

Praying with Persistence and Patience

You would think that we could pray for something once, and . . . boom. God's got it. We don't like it when people nag us about stuff, so we figure, "Hey, God heard me. He's not deaf."

No, God isn't deaf, but He does like to hear things more than once. We don't know why this is, but we think it has something to do with the fact that God loves to hear us talk to Him. Think of it this way. What if someone you care about very much were to say to you, "You are the greatest—there's no one like you." You would never respond by saying, "Thank you for the compliment, but never say that to me again." Instead, you would be inclined to say, "You know, I'm not sure I heard you correctly. Could you repeat that?"

That's the way God is. He hears our prayers, and He loves our prayers. In fact, He loves them so much that He wants us to repeat them over and over again. And if you don't think God plays favorites, think again. The Bible says that God rewards those who "diligently seek him" (Hebrews 11:6 KJV). It's always in our best interest to pray with persistence.

PERSISTENCE PAYS

Jesus told an amazing parable (read it for yourself in Luke 18:1-8) about a judge "who was a godless man with great contempt for everyone." There was a widow who lived in the same city who repeatedly appealed to the judge for justice against someone who had harmed her. The judge had no interest in helping the woman, but he finally gave in when she wore him out "with her constant requests." Jesus made the point that if a godless judge would answer a pleading woman, how much more would our God, who loves us, give justice "to his chosen people who plead with him day and night"!

Be Patient

We're coming to the end of our little book on prayer, and we've deliberately saved one of the most important principles of prayer until now. Are you ready? Here it is:

When you pray, wait patiently for God.

Waiting on the Lord is one of the hardest things you will ever do as a Christian. We want things and we want them now, but that's just not how God operates. We think our prayers go unanswered, but that's because our perspective is so limited. If only we could see with God's eyes and feel with God's heart. Then we would know how much He loves us, how much He wants for us, and how much He wants us to trust Him.

We need to trust that God will answer every prayer in the proper time and for our absolute good. We may not understand that now. We may never understand why God says "yes" to some things and "no" to others. But we can always trust Him to do the right thing.

To trust God is to put all of our weight on him. When we don't understand, when we hurt, when we suffer disappointment, when we are past asking for something or someone, when we feel

God is rarely early, never late, and always right on time.

*furious over the outcome—then
trusting God is finally just collapsing
in exhaustion on him. That is when
prayer comes back to its purest
meaning of* communion. *When we
are on the other side of asking we
simply come to God for who he is and
connect with him in the most basic
expression of faith.*

—Leith Anderson

"What's That Again?"

1. Praying with *power* means believing that God can do the impossible. If you want to move a mountain with your prayer, focus on God, not on the mountain.

2. Praying with *purpose* involves getting specific. Pray for people first, especially the lost. But when you pray for people to repent, pray first for yourself, and then for your fellow believers.

3. Praying with *passion* begins with intercessory prayer, which is pleading to God on behalf of other people. Jesus is interceding for you right now.

4. Praying with *persistence* is a key to success with God. Being *patient* in your praying means that you trust God completely.

Dig Deeper

In addition to the different Scripture passages we have suggested that you read (don't miss John 17), here are a few more books to add to your prayer reading list (as long as your reading isn't taking away from your praying).

- One of the writers on prayer is Evelyn Christenson. We found her book *A Time to Pray* very helpful in the area of learning how to pray for others, especially the lost. Christenson has been very involved in the AD 2000 Lighthouse Movement, an international prayer effort.

- We didn't have room to talk about prayer and fasting, but if that subject interests you, the classic book is *God's Chosen Fast* by Arthur Wallis.

- Nancie Carmichael's book *Desperate for God* will inspire you to turn your whole heart to God. Our goal should be to mature in our prayer life so that we are desperate for God.

Moving On

We've written a bunch of these guide books on some pretty important topics (like God, the Bible, and the end of the world). But nothing we have written so far has impacted us personally like this little book on prayer. Of course, it's not the book that's made the difference; it's the subject. We were overwhelmed with the truth that prayer is an awesome force in the life of the believer and in the world.

We hope—and we sincerely pray—that you have a similar feeling at this point. Like we said at the beginning of this book, what we say won't change your life. But the incredible power of prayer will transform you in ways you've only dreamed about. So what are you waiting for? Start talking to God. And while you're at it, tell Him we said hello.

Think About It

We certainly didn't say everything there is to know about prayer in these few pages, and you may still have a few questions. So do we, and here is a list of them. You can think about these questions, but thinking about answers to them might be even more helpful.

Chapter 1—Why Pray at All: Does It Really Make a Difference?

- Why does God want us talking to Him? He already knows what's going on in our lives, so He doesn't need information. What other reasons could there be?

- If God commands us to be praying, why are we so reluctant to do it?

- Do you agree that prayer "brings you into God's presence"? Do you notice any change in your feelings or attitudes when you pray?

- If you were talking to God right now, what are the circumstances in your life that you would want Him to change?

- What is it about *you* that you would want God to change?

Chapter 2—God Isn't a Web Site: There's More to Prayer Than Asking for Stuff

- What is it about talking to God that makes you uncomfortable? Make a list (be honest) and discuss it with someone you respect. Better yet, talk to God about it.

- What do you think God does with "desperate" prayers? These would be prayers offered by people who are in grave situations. Does it make any difference if the person praying has or hasn't opened his or her heart's door to Jesus?

- Give an example of what it means to pray outside the will of God.

- Jesus said that you can pray for anything. Do you really believe that? Can you think of anything that would be in God's will that you should *not* pray for?

**Chapter 3—What to Say When You Pray:
Do Words Really Matter?**

- Describe the content of your typical
  prayer. Do you have a pattern that you
  follow, or maybe a checklist, or do you
  use the stream-of-consciousness tech-
  nique?

- Review the Lord's Prayer. Take each
  phrase and describe, in your own
  words, the types of things Jesus was
  praying about.

- How does God speak to you? Are you
  listening for Him? What method do you
  use in your prayer time to give God a
  turn to talk?

- What's the "body language" that you
  use most often when you pray? Have
  you tried other ways to pray? If so, does
  one form work better than another? If
  not, what's keeping you from experi-
  menting?

Chapter 4—Pumped-Up Prayer: Talking to God with Power, Purpose, and Passion

- Give an example of something "impossible" you prayed for. What were the results?

- Who are the people you are most concerned about right now? What is it that worries you the most? Make a list and commit to pray for those people and things every day for the next week. At the end of the week, see what God has done with your list.

- How does knowing that Jesus is praying for you right now change the way you pray for other people?

- What's more difficult for you—persistence or patience?

About the Authors

Bruce Bickel is a lawyer, but he didn't start out that bad. After college, he considered the noble profession of a stand-up comic, but he had to abandon that dream because he is not very funny. As a lawyer, he makes people laugh (but it is not on purpose).

Stan Jantz is a retail-marketing consultant. From the time he was a little kid, Stan's family owned a chain of Christian bookstores, so he feels very comfortable behind the counter.

Bruce and Stan spend their free time as "cultural observers" (they made that term up). They watch how God applies to real life. Together they have written 20 books, and they host a weekly radio program, *The Bruce & Stan Show*. (Gee, you've got to wonder how they came up with that catchy title.)

Other Books by the Guys:

Bruce & Stan's Guide to God
Bruce & Stan's Guide to the Bible
Bruce & Stan's Guide to the End of the World
Bruce & Stan's Pocket Guide to Sharing Your Faith
God Is in the Small Stuff (and It All Matters)
God Is in the Small Stuff for Your Family
God Is in the Small Stuff for Your Marriage
Onyourown.com—e-mail messages to my daughter
Real Life Begins After High School

Bruce and Stan would enjoy hearing from you. (If you've got something nice to say, then don't hold back. If you have a criticism, then be gentle.) The best way to contact them is:

E-mail: **guide@bruceandstan.com**
Snail Mail: Bruce & Stan
P.O. Box 25565 Fresno, CA 93729-5565

You can learn more than you ever wanted to know about Bruce and Stan by visiting their Web site: **www.bruceandstan.com**